The Little Book of

NORTH AMERICAN TREES

**BUSHEL
& PECK
BOOKS**

Bushel & Peck Books is dedicated to fighting illiteracy all over the world.
For every book we sell, we donate one to a child in need——book for book.
To nominate a school or organization to receive free books,
please visit www.bushelandpeckbooks.com.

Type set in Temeraire, Avenir Next, and Bebas.

Illustrations sourced from the Biodiversity Heritage Library, Wikimedia Commons,
and The Graphics Fairy. Other image credits as follows: vine pattern: Nespola Designs/
Shutterstock.com; graph paper background: Vector Image Plus/Shutterstock.com.
Taxonomy sourced from Wikipedia.

ISBN: 9781638191568

First Edition

Printed in the United States

10 9 8 7 6 5 4 3 2 1

The Little Book of
NORTH AMERICAN TREES

CHRISTIN FARLEY

Contents

NATIVE NECESSITIES

Red maple bark had many everyday uses for Native Americans. The inner bark was brewed for tea to treat coughs and diarrhea. It was also used as an analgesic to relieve muscular pain and hives.

1. RED MAPLE

While there are over 120 species of maple trees worldwide, only thirteen are native to North America. The red maple is a common eye-catcher, especially in the fall when its green leaves turn a bright red hue. Recognized as one of the most abundant native trees in Eastern North America, the red maple has many human uses. Crates, musical instruments, paper, and furniture can all be made from red maple's fine-grained wood. Even sweeter is the sap of the red maple, which can be used to make syrup. With a healthy lifespan of about 100 years and heavy seed production, we can expect hosts of red maples for generations to come!

CLASSIFICATION

KINGDOM: *Plantae*

CLADE: *Tracheophytes*

CLADE: *Angiosperms*

CLADE: *Eudicots*

CLADE: *Rosids*

ORDER: *Sapindales*

FAMILY: *Sapindaceae*

GENUS: *Acer*

SPECIES: *A. rubrum*

QUICK FACTS

TREE TYPE	*Deciduous*
LEAF ARRANGEMENT	*Opposite*
BARK DESCRIPTION	*Light gray and smooth but develops cracks and raised edges as it ages*
NATIVE OR INVASIVE	*Native*

WINGED WONDERS

The seeds of maple trees are often referred to as "helicopters" due to their signature twirling as they fall from trees each year. The seed is actually encased in a two-winged structure called a "samara," allowing it to fly through the air.

ANIMAL FRIENDLY

In addition to being incredibly interesting, quaking aspens are indispensable to their environment. Moose, elk, and deer seek refuge under the shade of aspen groves in the summer while consuming their bark, leaves, and twigs year-round.

2. QUAKING ASPEN

The quaking aspen is aptly named—the tree's long, flat stems cause the leaves to shake in a light breeze. As hardy trees, quaking aspens can grow from Alaska all the way to Mexico, where they grow at lower altitudes in the north and higher altitudes in the south. An identifying characteristic is their unique white bark. Unlike most trees, the bark carries out the process of photosynthesis instead of the leaves! And if that wasn't astonishing enough, individual aspen trees usually sprout from an existing root structure called a "clone." Such groups of trees with the same root system can live for tens of thousands of years!

CLASSIFICATION

KINGDOM: *Plantae*

CLADE: *Tracheophytes*

CLADE: *Angiosperms*

CLADE: *Eudicots*

CLADE: *Rosids*

ORDER: *Malpighiales*

FAMILY: *Salicaceae*

GENUS: *Populus*

SECTION: *Populus sect. Populus*

SPECIES: *P. tremuloides*

QUICK FACTS

TREE TYPE	*Deciduous*
LEAF ARRANGEMENT	*Alternate*
BARK DESCRIPTION	*Smooth, grayish-white bark that grows rougher with age*
NATIVE OR INVASIVE	*Native*

LARGER THAN LIFE

The largest living organism by mass on Earth is a group of quaking aspen trees in Utah called "Pando." It is a single underground root system that produces almost 50,000 stems (trees), weighing 6,000 tons and covering over 100 acres!

9

FANS OF FIRES

Forest fires play a crucial role in the reproduction of giant sequoias. Seeds can remain in their cones for 20 years until a forest fire comes to help open the cones. From there, the seeds can then sprout in the bare and burnt forest soil.

3. GIANT SEQUOIA

I f knowledge comes with age, then giant sequoias would have to be some of the wisest trees on Earth! With lifespans of over 3,000 years, they have had a front-row seat to much of Earth's changes over time. These giants make their home on the western slopes of the Sierra Nevada mountain range, where natural growth only occurs in a 260-mile strip of forest. Sequoias have specific climate requirements that limit them to elevations of 5,000 to 7,000 feet. While they were logged for wood in the early days of California, giant sequoias are now a protected tree species.

CLASSIFICATION

KINGDOM: *Plantae*

CLADE: *Gymnosperms*

DIVISION: *Pinophyta*

CLASS: *Pinopsida*

ORDER: *Cupressales*

FAMILY: *Cupressaceae*

GENUS: *Sequoiadendron*

SPECIES: *S. giganteum*

QUICK FACTS

TREE TYPE	*Coniferous*
LEAF ARRANGEMENT	*Round, prickly needles with an overlapping shingle arrangement*
BARK DESCRIPTION	*Soft, brownish-red bark that is fire, pest, rot, and fungi-resistant and can exceed a foot in thickness*
NATIVE OR INVASIVE	*Native*

CLAIM TO FAME

The Sequoia National Park in California is home to the famous General Sherman Tree. It is known as the largest tree in the world (by volume) with a height of 275 feet and a diameter of 36 feet!

11

HISTORIC HABITAT

A southern magnolia was planted on the White House grounds by Andrew Jackson, the 7th President of the United States. It thrived for more than 200 years on the grounds until 2017, when it was no longer healthy.

4. SOUTHERN MAGNOLIA

Though they can be cultivated all over the globe, southern magnolia trees are native to the southeastern part of the United States. It's hard to miss the elegant, white, aromatic flowers and large, glossy leaves of a southern magnolia. These medium- to large-sized trees have shallow roots and, therefore, need soil that is consistently moist. This moisture limitation does not seem to affect southern magnolia growth, however, as they can reach up to 90 feet in height and live to be 120 years old! A crowd pleaser, it's hard not to love a southern magnolia it's even the state tree for Mississippi and Louisiana!

CLASSIFICATION

KINGDOM: *Plantae*

CLADE: *Angiosperms*

CLADE: *Magnoliids*

ORDER: *Magnoliales*

FAMILY: *Magnoliaceae*

GENUS: *Magnolia*

SECTION: *Magnolia sect. Magnolia*

SPECIES: *M. grandiflora*

QUICK FACTS

TREE TYPE	*Evergreen*
LEAF ARRANGEMENT	*Alternate*
BARK DESCRIPTION	*Shades of gray, smooth texture with small lenticels (allows for gas exchange)*
NATIVE OR INVASIVE	*Native*

FUN FACTS

Leaves of the southern magnolia can grow up to 8 inches long, while the brilliant flowers can reach 12 inches in diameter. Also, if a magnolia branch becomes crushed or injured, that section of the tree will release a citrus-like scent.

13

BAD BAD BEETLES

The emerald ash borer beetle poses a threat to green ash trees. They were accidentally introduced to the United States from Asia. The high tannin content in the leaves of Asain varieties makes them undesirable to the beetles. However, American ash trees are susceptible without the same tannin levels.

5. GREEN ASH

Green ash trees have the widest distribution of all the American ash varieties. They can be found as far north as Nova Scotia, Canada, and as far south as Texas and Florida in the United States. Their ability to thrive in a wide range of soil conditions makes them a popular choice for planting. Known for its strong and durable lumber, green ash wood is used to manufacture many popular items such as tool handles and baseball bats. Clusters of purple and green flowers without petals that bloom in spring are a key clue that you have found a green ash! In the fall, the medium-sized green leaves turn a vibrant yellow.

CLASSIFICATION

KINGDOM: *Plantae*

CLADE: *Angiosperms*

CLADE: *Eudicots*

CLADE: *Asterids*

ORDER: *Lamiales*

FAMILY: *Oleaceae*

GENUS: *Fraxinus*

SECTION: *Fraxinus sect. Melioides*

SPECIES: *F. pennsylvanica*

QUICK FACTS

TREE TYPE	*Deciduous*
LEAF ARRANGEMENT	*Opposite*
BARK DESCRIPTION	*Smooth when young, develops fissures and distinct ridges as it ages*
NATIVE OR INVASIVE	*Native*

ROCK ON!

Green ash wood is a highly desirable wood variety when constructing electric guitars. The wood grain is aesthetically pleasing and has a good musical tone. Guitar brands like Warwick, Fender, and Gibson are known to use ash wood.

PIONEER PREFERENCE

How did the tulip tree become the state tree of Tennessee? It was for its historic significance, as it was commonly used by pioneers in the early days to make canoes, barns, and houses.

6. AMERICAN TULIP

Due to its popularity, the tulip tree has many titles. It is known as the "yellow poplar" in the lumber industry (though it is actually part of the magnolia family). In Tennessee, it is affectionately referred to as "canoe wood," as early settlers made canoes from its lightweight and buoyant trunk. It is also known as the tallest of the American hardwood trees, reaching heights of about 100 feet. Perhaps what it is best known for, however, is its tulip-shaped flowers that emerge in the spring. May and early June are the perfect months to see firsthand the stunningly large yellow and orange blooms!

CLASSIFICATION

KINGDOM:KINGDOM: *Plantae*

CLADE: *Tracheophytes*

CLADE: *Angiosperms*

CLADE: *Magnoliids*

ORDER: *Magnoliales*

FAMILY: *Magnoliaceae*

GENUS: *Liriodendron*

SPECIES: *L. tulipifera*

QUICK FACTS

TREE TYPE	*Deciduous*
LEAF ARRANGEMENT	*Alternate*
BARK DESCRIPTION	*Smooth and dark when young, developing deep grooves with age*
NATIVE OR INVASIVE	*Native*

HISTORICAL HIGHLIGHTS

The first U.S. President, George Washington, admired the tulip tree. He chose this variety to be known as Mount Vernon's official Bicentennial Tree in 1785.

17

18

7. AMERICAN SYCAMORE

American sycamores are nostalgic parts of early American history. Sturdy and hardy, sycamores can survive up to 600 years in the wild and are commonly found in the eastern deciduous forests. Much of America's defining moments in history occurred here. Firm and immovable, sycamores serve as windbreaks with strong root systems, and they are tolerant of almost any soil conditions. As a result, they are as popular in urban areas today as they were historically when they provided vast amounts of shade to early settlers. The brown woody seed balls that emerge in October are a defining characteristic of the American sycamore. Such fruits release around 10,000 seeds per year.

CLASSIFICATION

KINGDOM: *Plantae*

CLADE: *Tracheophytes*

CLADE: *Angiosperms*

CLADE: *Eudicots*

ORDER: *Proteales*

FAMILY: *Platanaceae*

GENUS: *Platanus*

SPECIES: *P. occidentalis*

QUICK FACTS

TREE TYPE	*Deciduous*
LEAF ARRANGEMENT	*Alternate*
BARK DESCRIPTION	*Sheds bark in irregular pieces, leaving mottled patches of gray, green, and brown*
NATIVE OR INVASIVE	*Native*

BUTTONBALL BEAUTY

Sutherland, Massachusetts is the home to the famed "Buttonball Tree." This American sycamore is famous for its size and longevity. Believed to be well over 350 years old, it has a girth of almost 26 feet and is known by the locals as, "The widest tree this side of the Mississippi."

USEFUL USES

Paper birch trees provide many benefits to the environment. They are a source of food for more than 30 different kinds of birds and mammals. In need of a campfire? No problem! Paper birch tree wood can burn at high temperatures— even if the wood is wet!

8. PAPER BIRCH

With their peeling white bark, paper birch trees are breathtakingly beautiful against dark backgrounds and rural landscapes. Native to the colder climates of the Northeastern United States and Canada, paper birch trees make their homes along lakesides and stream banks. With a narrow canopy and tall heights of around 60 feet, grass and ground cover can easily grow underneath. They do not fare as well in a city atmosphere with greater heat, dry conditions, and pollution. Heavy snow and wind can also break branches. Even with these limitations, paper birch trees are highly popular. They represent New Hampshire as the state tree and are the provincial tree of Saskatchewan.

CLASSIFICATION

KINGDOM: *Plantae*

CLADE: *Angiosperms*

CLADE: *Eudicots*

CLADE: *Rosids*

ORDER: *Fagales*

FAMILY: *Betulaceae*

GENUS: *Betula*

SUBGENUS: *Betula subg. Betula*

SPECIES: *B. papyrifera*

QUICK FACTS

TREE TYPE	*Deciduous*
LEAF ARRANGEMENT	*Alternate*
BARK DESCRIPTION	*Reddish-brown when young, turns white and peels off like paper when it grows old*
NATIVE OR INVASIVE	*Native*

MODERN USES

Many everyday items you might purchase at the store could be made of paper birch trees. Toothpicks, bobbins, broom handles, and ice cream sticks are often made from birch. Hobby crafters also use thin bark strips for creating decorations.

FURNITURE, NOT FOOD

Yes, you can eat the fruit of a black cherry tree. However, you might find it too bitter to enjoy. Black cherries are used in jams and pies more than they are eaten fresh. Instead, the black cherry tree is prized for its lumber, as it is highly desirable for flooring and furniture making.

2

9. BLACK CHERRY

Japan is not the only place to see cherry blossoms. From Southern Canada down to Florida and Texas, black cherry trees are a common yet splendid find! In fact, springtime in Washington, D.C., is famous for its spectacular show of blossoms! As a result, the black cherry is a popular tree choice in public areas, gardens, and parks. Medium to large in size, they can grow to be around 50-60 feet tall with a common diameter of 2 feet. Black cherry trees can produce fruit until they reach 170 years of age, though production doesn't begin until age 10. Look for fruit ripening in late August through September!

CLASSIFICATION

KINGDOM: *Plantae*

CLADE: *Angiosperms*

CLADE: *Eudicots*

CLADE: *Rosids*

ORDER: *Rosales*

FAMILY: *Rosaceae*

GENUS: *Prunus*

SUBGENUS: *Prunus subg. Padus*

SPECIES: *P. serotina*

QUICK FACTS

COWS KEEP OUT!

While black cherry trees seem harmless, their leaves, bark, and twigs can pose a credible threat to livestock. The wilted leaves of cherry trees are especially lethal as they contain high doses of hydrogen cyanide. Severe intoxication and/or death can occur from consuming a pound of leaves in a short time.

TREE TYPE	*Deciduous*
LEAF ARRANGEMENT	*Alternate*
BARK DESCRIPTION	*Dark gray, thin and smooth until reaching 10 years of age; stiff and scaly as it ages*
NATIVE OR INVASIVE	*Native*

23

NATIVE NAME

The Southern United States is the home of the native
Muscogee people, also known as the "Creek." Roughly
translated into English, the Muscogee word for "tupelo" is
"swamp tree," which accurately describes the region where the
water tupelo tree originates.

10. WATER TUPELO

Also known as "cotton gum" or "swamp gum," the water tupelo is a member of the dogwood family. As its name implies, the water tupelo is an aquatic tree found in swamps or near other bodies of water. Their roots often grow out of the water while their trunks, swollen at the base, thin out as they reach heights of up to 100 feet. Water tupelo trees produce a dark, reddish-purple fruit that provides food for local deer, wood ducks, and squirrels. This long-lived variety (which can live up to 1000 years!) is popular among bee pollinators, who consume its nectar and make Tupelo honey.

CLASSIFICATION

KINGDOM: *Plantae*

CLADE: *Tracheophytes*

CLADE: *Angiosperms*

CLADE: *Eudicots*

CLADE: *Asterids*

ORDER: *Cornales*

FAMILY: *Nyssaceae*

GENUS: *Nyssa*

SPECIES: *N. aquatica*

QUICK FACTS

TREE TYPE	*Deciduous*
LEAF ARRANGEMENT	*Alternate*
BARK DESCRIPTION	*Dark brown or gray with fissures*
NATIVE OR INVASIVE	*Native*

DECOY DELIGHT

The light wood of water tupelo trees is used to make plywood, boxes, crates, paper pulp, and furniture. Woodcarvers are especially fond of the swollen timber of the lower trunk. Its buoyant properties and tendency to not split allow woodcarvers to easily make duck decoys.

WILD AND FREE

Unlike their cousin, the English walnut, black walnuts are neither processed by hand nor grown in orchards. Black walnuts are the only all-wild nut tree in the United States. The majority of the trees are found in Missouri and are rare in comparison to other types of walnut trees.

11. BLACK WALNUT

Native to North America, black walnut trees are widely popular for their beauty and timber. Reaching heights of over 75 feet, their canopies often reach out in equal measure, providing plenty of shade. Black walnut trees produce delicious nuts with extremely hard shells that are edible after a curing process. Their health benefits and distinctive flavor make the nuts highly desirable. Equally attractive is black walnut wood. Trunks are generally tall and free of branches, making them ideal for timber uses. With their rich coloring, fine graining, and ease of workability, black walnuts are a premier North American hardwood.

CLASSIFICATION

KINGDOM: *Plantae*

CLADE: *Angiosperms*

CLADE: *Eudicots*

CLADE: *Rosids*

ORDER: *Fagales*

FAMILY: *Juglandaceae*

GENUS: *Juglans*

SECTION: *Juglans sect. Rhysocaryon*

SPECIES: *J. nigra*

QUICK FACTS

TREE TYPE	*Deciduous*
LEAF ARRANGEMENT	*Alternate*
BARK DESCRIPTION	*Thick and dark grayish-black with deep grooves*
NATIVE OR INVASIVE	*Native*

KEEPING ITS DISTANCE

Black walnut trees are not fond of competition from other plant life. Their roots, which can reach out to 50 feet, exude a natural herbicide known as "juglone." Such a substance inhibits the growth of plants in its vicinity, therefore keeping nutrients for itself!

HOME SWEET HOME

The old fronds that form the palm skirt can be unsightly to some and are often trimmed in residential areas. However, for many creatures, the dead leaves provide a perfectly suitable habitat. An entire ecosystem of birds, insects, and small rodents exists from the bottom of the skirt to the top of the tree.

12. CALIFORNIA FAN PALM

California fan palms are also known as the "desert fan" palm, the "American cotton" palm, and the "Arizona fan" palm. The name is representative of the palm's natural habitat. This flowering palm inhabits areas of the Southwestern United States and Baja, California. Of the thirteen palm species native to the continental United States, the California palm's long skirt is easy to spot. Instead of falling off, dead palm fronds turn gray and bend downward around the tall, lean trunk. One of the benefits of this palm variety is the relatively low maintenance it requires. Being drought-tolerant, cold hardy, and fire-resistant, it's no wonder the fan palm is a popular California choice!

CLASSIFICATION

KINGDOM: *Plantae*

CLADE: *Angiosperms*

CLADE: *Monocots*

CLADE: *Commelinids*

ORDER: *Arecales*

FAMILY: *Arecaceae*

TRIBE: *Trachycarpeae*

GENUS: *Washingtonia*

SPECIES: *W. filifera*

QUICK FACTS

TREE TYPE	*Evergreen*
LEAF ARRANGEMENT	*Palmate (lobes radiating from a common point)*
BARK DESCRIPTION	*They do not have bark*
NATIVE OR INVASIVE	*Native—the only palm native to Western North America*

NATURE'S SUGAR

If you like fruit, you should try the fruit of a fan palm. The small, berry-like fruits are black in color and emerge in September after flowering. They can be eaten fresh or boiled to be used as a syrup or a natural sweetener.

29

CLOSE TIES

It might be surprising to learn that a tree so tall has shallow roots that measure only 6-12 feet in depth. What they lack in depth, they make up for in breadth. These roots can extend up to 100 feet from the base while intertwining with the roots of other redwoods for added strength.

13. GIANT REDWOOD (COAST REDWOOD)

From Big Sur, California, up north to parts of Southern Oregon, you have a chance to see groves of the tallest trees in the world, not to mention some of the most ancient. Coastal redwoods are a sight to behold if you can actually see their tops at over 300 feet. They are so famous that the exact locations of the tallest trees are kept a secret to protect them from humans. While smaller in mass than their giant sequoia cousins, coastal redwoods are similar in that they have tiny pinecones in comparison to their size. Their inch-long cones only house a few dozen minute seeds.

RESOURCEFUL REDWOODS

Like most California trees in winter, redwoods get their moisture from rainwater. When summer rolls around, redwoods have to be more resourceful. The fog that rolls in from the Pacific coast accounts for about 40% of their water intake when it accumulates on needles and is absorbed by the trees.

CLASSIFICATION

KINGDOM: *Plantae*

CLADE: *Gymnosperms*

DIVISION: *Pinophyta*

CLASS: *Pinopsida*

ORDER: *Cupressales*

FAMILY: *Cupressaceae*

GENUS: *Sequoia*

SPECIES: *S. sempervirens*

QUICK FACTS

TREE TYPE	*Coniferous evergreen*
LEAF ARRANGEMENT	*Flat needles that only grow out of the sides of branches*
BARK DESCRIPTION	*Up to 12 inches thick, reddish-brown, and pest repellant*
NATIVE OR INVASIVE	*Native only to the Pacific coast of California and Oregon*

Redbud tree blossoms are actually purple and vibrant in color. Such pigmentation makes for a bright addition to salads, as the buds are edible. They have a citrusy flavor and can be both pickled and used as a substitute for capers in recipes (if the buds are unopened).

14. EASTERN REDBUD

Redbud trees are small in size (only 15-30 feet tall) and are known for their fragrant flowers and heart-shaped leaves. They are the state tree of Oklahoma and have special significance to the people of Israel, where they are protected. Redbuds have a relatively short lifespan of 35-45 years as they are susceptible to pests and fungal infections. Besides being a lovely ornamental choice, redbuds have many everyday uses. For instance, their roots contain substances that help produce red dye. Redbud hardwood is used to make veneers. Their fruit pods also contain black seeds that are a common staple in the diets of birds and deer.

CLASSIFICATION

KINGDOM: *Plantae*

CLADE: *Tracheophytes*

CLADE: *Angiosperms*

CLADE: *Eudicots*

CLADE: *Rosids*

ORDER: *Fabales*

FAMILY: *Fabaceae*

GENUS: *Cercis*

SPECIES: *C. canadensis*

QUICK FACTS

TREE TYPE	*Deciduous*
LEAF ARRANGEMENT	*Alternate*
BARK DESCRIPTION	*Smooth and gray when young, becomes coarse and scaly with age*
NATIVE OR INVASIVE	*Native*

CAULIFLORY?

While the term "cauliflory" sounds like a vegetable, it is actually a phenomenon that occurs in the resplendent redbud. Buds not only appear on the bark of twigs and branches, but they also grow in mini clusters from the trunk.

33

SUPERFOOD

As one of the most nutritious nuts, pecans contain 19 vitamins and minerals, not to mention fats, fiber, protein, amino acids, starch, and sugars. An added bonus is that the fat content is mostly monounsaturated and can help lower bad LDL cholesterol.

15. PECAN

It's been said that it takes a magnificent tree to produce a magnificent nut, and this is definitely true of a pecan tree! Pecan trees are not only known for their quality of wood (and expense) but are remarkably fruitful as well. It takes around 12 years for pecan trees to produce, but once they start, they can be productive for over 200 years! The commercial production of pecans in the United States began in the early 1900s, and now the country produces about 80% of the world's pecans. Georgia is the top pecan producer in the U.S., followed by Texas. In fact, Texas is such a big fan that it named the pecan its state tree!

CLASSIFICATION

KINGDOM: *Plantae*

CLADE: *Angiosperms*

CLADE: *Eudicots*

CLADE: *Rosids*

ORDER: *Fagales*

FAMILY: *Juglandaceae*

GENUS: *Carya*

SECTION: *Carya sect. Apocarya*

SPECIES: *C. illinoinensis*

QUICK FACTS

TREE TYPE	*Deciduous*
LEAF ARRANGEMENT	*Alternate*
BARK DESCRIPTION	*Rough, gray, and scaly bark, known to shed in large amounts*
NATIVE OR INVASIVE	*Native*

PRE-AMERICAN PECAN

Long before English colonization, pecans were cultivated and consumed by natives of America and Mexico. The word "pecan" comes from the native Algonquin language used to describe "all nuts requiring a stone to crack." They were a main food source in the fall season.

SPECTACULAR SHOWING

People from all over the globe are known to visit the northeastern parts of the U.S. to view the spectacular fall foliage. Sassafras trees do not disappoint as their leaves turn from green to yellow, orange, red, and finally purple before they fall.

16. SASSAFRAS

Of all the trees in North America, the sassafras has to be one of the most unique! Unlike other tree species, sassafras leaves can exhibit three different appearances! Leaves can be oval-shaped, two-lobed, or three-lobed. In extremely rare cases, leaves with four or five lobes have also been found! Located in eastern parts of the United States and Southern Canada, sassafras can grow as a tall shrub or tree, reaching heights of up to 60 feet. Known as "pioneer species," sassafras trees are some of the first trees to pop up after fires, floods, or landslides, as they can handle soils with low pH levels.

CLASSIFICATION

KINGDOM: *Plantae*

CLADE: *Tracheophytes*

CLADE: *Angiosperms*

CLADE: *Magnoliids*

ORDER: *Laurales*

FAMILY: *Lauraceae*

GENUS: *Sassafras*

SPECIES: *S. albidum*

EDIBLE AND DISTINCTIVE

When twigs, leaves, or roots of the sassafras are crushed, a distinctive aroma is released, making the tree easy to identify. Some people say that the roots smell like root beer, while others comment that their bark and leaves smell like Froot Loops cereal! As an added bonus, the twigs and leaves are edible!

QUICK FACTS

TREE TYPE	*Deciduous*
LEAF ARRANGEMENT	*Alternate*
BARK DESCRIPTION	*Smooth and green when young, becomes furrowed and reddish-brown with age*
NATIVE OR INVASIVE	*Native*

AGGRESSIVE ROOTS

Like the fast-growing trunk and branches, homeowners need to be aware of the strong and aggressive root system of weeping willows. They can reach far beyond the scope of the tree itself, wreaking havoc on underground water, gas, sewage, and electric lines!

17. WEEPING WILLOW

Weeping willows are an iconic tree species known for their beauty and use in modern and classic literature. Its namesake comes from the way raindrops run down the elongated leaves, making it appear as though it is crying. Thankfully, there is nothing sad about a weeping willow except for its short lifespan of about 30 years. One of the amazing features of this willow is that it can reproduce without any fertilization! Known as "vegetative reproduction," weeping willows can sprout new growth from the fragments of the parent plant. This means that you can clip a healthy branch and replant it somewhere else, and it will begin to take root in a few weeks!

CLASSIFICATION

KINGDOM: *Plantae*

CLADE: *Tracheophytes*

CLADE: *Angiosperms*

CLADE: *Eudicots*

CLADE: *Rosids*

ORDER: *Malpighiales*

FAMILY: *Salicaceae*

GENUS: *Salix*

SPECIES: *S. babylonica*

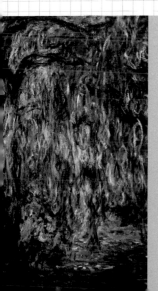

FAST PACED

If weeping willows could run, they would be sprinters! Once they have been established for around 3 years, they turn up the speed and grow up to 10 feet per year! This is much faster than many other tree varieties.

QUICK FACTS

TREE TYPE	*Deciduous*
LEAF ARRANGEMENT	*Alternate*
BARK DESCRIPTION	*Gray or dark brown, scaly and furrowed*
NATIVE OR INVASIVE	*Common in North America but native to North China*

OUCH!

The spikes on the gumballs will definitely get your attention if you step on them by accident! But their texture serves an important purpose. The spikes easily stick to animal fur and are, therefore, transported to new places to release the inner seeds and grow new sweetgums!

18. SWEETGUM

You can pinpoint a sweetgum tree by its distinctive star-shaped leaves and spiky fruit, or "gumballs!" Its name comes from the gummy sap that oozes from the wounds of the tree. While it doesn't taste like bubblegum, the resin can be chewed and was one of the earliest versions of modern chewing gum. Sweetgum trees are commonly found in the southeastern parts of the United States and Mexico. A popular choice for reforestation projects, sweetgum trees are fast-growing and highly resistant to insects. In addition, sweetgums are often planted to help fix nitrogen levels and restore soil health.

CLASSIFICATION

KINGDOM: *Plantae*

CLADE: *Tracheophytes*

CLADE: *Angiosperms*

CLADE: *Eudicots*

ORDER: *Saxifragales*

FAMILY: *Altingiaceae*

GENUS: *Liquidambar*

SPECIES: *L. styraciflua*

QUICK FACTS

TREE TYPE	*Deciduous*
LEAF ARRANGEMENT	*Alternate*
BARK DESCRIPTION	*Gray or brown with rough ridges and irregular furrows*
NATIVE OR INVASIVE	*Native*

DENTIST APPROVED

Dental hygiene was important hundreds of years ago, just as it is today. Native Americans used the resin from sweetgum trees to eliminate bacteria from the mouth, as the resin has antiseptic properties.

41

CANKER CRISIS

Butternut canker is a fungus that kills healthy butternuts of any age. Difficult to treat and control, the disease starts under the bark and grows to surround the branches, restricting water and nutrient flow. Some areas of the U.S. have lost 90% of their butternut trees to the fungus.

19. BUTTERNUT

Also known as the "white walnut," butternut trees are found in the New England states of the United States and as far northwest as Minnesota. Butternuts are known for their sweet and buttery nuts that resemble the shape of a butternut squash (hence the name). They tend to grow as individual trees instead of in clusters and are usually found near other hardwood varieties. Butternuts are intolerant of shade and need full sun, along with cooler temperatures at higher elevations. While its lumber is stable with very little cracking and warping, it is not in high demand. Butternuts are soft and good for carving but are rarely in commercial supply.

CLASSIFICATION

KINGDOM: *Plantae*

CLADE: *Angiosperms*

CLADE: *Eudicots*

CLADE: *Rosids*

ORDER: *Fagales*

FAMILY: *Juglandaceae*

GENUS: *Juglans*

SECTION: *Juglans sect. Trachycaryon*

SPECIES: *J. cinerea*

QUICK FACTS

TREE TYPE	*Deciduous*
LEAF ARRANGEMENT	*Opposite*
BARK DESCRIPTION	*Light gray with a rough, fissured texture*
NATIVE OR INVASIVE	*Native*

TASTY TREATS

With a high oil content, butternuts make a great addition to dessert foods. Butternuts are a popular choice in the New England states, as they are a great complement to maple flavors and help produce delicious maple-butternut candies!

SUN STEALERS

If you plant an American beech tree, think twice about adding more vegetation nearby. Beech leaves don't allow much sunlight to reach organisms below them. A shallow root system that stretches out beneath the beech also inhibits the growth and productivity of other plants.

20. AMERICAN BEECH

The American beech is a versatile tree that is widely used in the forestry industry; on top of this, it is planted for the beauty and shade it provides in parks and golf courses. In the wild, they can reach heights of 100 feet, while the standard size in residential landscapes can reach upwards of 50 feet. Intolerant of high levels of carbon monoxide, beeches do well in suburban areas. The greatest distribution of American beech trees is in Eastern North America, where there is plenty of rainfall and well-drained soil. Its edible nuts are a major food source for wildlife like squirrels, black bears, white-tailed deer, wild turkeys, and foxes.

CLASSIFICATION

KINGDOM: *Plantae*

CLADE: *Tracheophytes*

CLADE: *Angiosperms*

CLADE: *Eudicots*

CLADE: *Rosids*

ORDER: *Fagales*

FAMILY: *Fagaceae*

GENUS: *Fagus*

SPECIES: *F. grandifolia*

BEECH FOR BUILDING?

Yes, beech wood can be a great choice for craftsmen. However, this odorless hardwood has one disadvantage. Because they absorb a lot of moisture, they are not a good material to use in high-humidity areas, like near the sea. Hours of hard work and woodcrafting can be destroyed quickly in wet environments!

QUICK FACTS

TREE TYPE	*Deciduous*
LEAF ARRANGEMENT	*Alternate*
BARK DESCRIPTION	*Smooth throughout its life, light gray in color*
NATIVE OR INVASIVE	*Native*

Noble firs can live long lives if forests are spared of logging and fires. Though extremely rare, noble firs can even reach over 600 years of age. The oldest known noble fir lived for 600 to 700 years. Under optimal conditions, their typical life spans are around 400 years.

21. NOBLE FIR

Nothing says Christmas like a noble fir! The blue-green needles, perfectly spaced branches, and rich fragrance are what make the "King" of Christmas trees stand out. In the wild, noble firs can grow over 200 feet tall—a surprise when compared to their typical holiday heights of 8-10 feet. As the largest native fir in North America, this noble features a conical crown, a long columnar trunk, and an overall pyramidal shape. They are native to the Cascade and coastal regions of Oregon and Washington, along with the Siskiyou Mountains of California. Here, they thrive with at least 4 hours of full sun and soil that is deep, moist, acidic, and well-drained.

CLASSIFICATION

KINGDOM: *Plantae*

CLADE: *Tracheophytes*

CLADE: *Gymnosperms*

DIVISION: *Pinophyta*

CLASS: *Pinopsida*

ORDER: *Pinales*

FAMILY: *Pinaceae*

GENUS: *Abies*

SPECIES: *A. procera*

ENVIRONMENTALLY FRIENDLY

Did you know that Christmas tree farms are actually helpful for the environment? These man-made forests provide ecological benefits by taking in carbon dioxide and releasing oxygen. Real trees do not end up in landfills and can be recycled into mulch at the end of their use. In addition, tree farmers replant 1-3 seeds in place of every tree harvested.

QUICK FACTS

TREE TYPE	*Coniferous*
LEAF ARRANGEMENT	*Needles are arranged spirally on the shoot*
BARK DESCRIPTION	*Gray and smooth when young, reddish-brown and rough with age*
NATIVE OR INVASIVE	*Native*

OLD-GROWTH GONE

Extensive logging from the 18th to early 20th centuries took an excessive toll on the eastern white pine forests of the United States. Such forests originally covered most of the north-central and northeastern parts of North America. Today, however, only 1% of the old-growth forests remain.

22. EASTERN WHITE PINE

Like its name implies, the eastern white pine is found on the eastern side of North America, as far north as Newfoundland, Canada, and as far south as Georgia. Not only is it the state tree of Michigan, but it was also once the state's lumber staple when it led the lumber industry in the 1800s. White pine trees are commonly grown for Christmas trees and are used in the production of flooring, doors, and cabinetry. Part of the value and appeal of the white pine is its soft wood, making it easier to work with, and it has fewer knots when compared to other conifer trees.

CLASSIFICATION

KINGDOM: *Plantae*

CLADE: *Gymnosperms*

DIVISION: *Pinophyta*

CLASS: *Pinopsida*

ORDER: *Pinales*

FAMILY: *Pinaceae*

GENUS: *Pinus*

SUBGENUS: *P. subg. Strobus*

SPECIES: *P. strobus*

QUICK FACTS

TREE TYPE	*Coniferous*
LEAF ARRANGEMENT	*Soft, slender needles grown in clusters of five*
BARK DESCRIPTION	*Dark green and smooth when young, dark gray and ridged when mature*
NATIVE OR INVASIVE	*Native*

TEAM PLAYERS

Eastern white pine trees help clean our air, and they provide many benefits to their animal neighbors. While it can be damaging to the tree, beavers, porcupines, and rabbits consume the pine's bark. Many birds, like woodpeckers and chickadees, also take advantage of the trees as nesting sites.

COUSINS ACROSS CONTINENTS

The three major species of mulberry trees are red, white, and black mulberries. While the red mulberry is native to North America, the white and black species originated in Asia. Historically, the main use of the Asian varieties was to grow food for the silkworm industry.

23. **RED MULBERRY**

Reaching heights of up to 70 feet, the red mulberry is the largest of the genus Morus. As a medium-sized tree, the red mulberry is desirable for its shade and ornamental beauty. The most defining characteristic of the tree is its fruit. Large in size and black when ripe, the fruit of a red mulberry is comparable in appearance to a blackberry (though its taste is very different). Like humans, small mammals and birds also enjoy the rich fruit the tree provides. The relatively short trunk grows about 2 feet in diameter and is a generally accepted choice in making barrels and fence posts.

CLASSIFICATION

KINGDOM: *Plantae*

CLADE: *Tracheophytes*

CLADE: *Angiosperms*

CLADE: *Eudicots*

CLADE: *Rosids*

ORDER: *Rosales*

FAMILY: *Moraceae*

GENUS: *Morus*

SPECIES: *M. rubra*

QUICK FACTS

TREE TYPE	*Deciduous*
LEAF ARRANGEMENT	*Alternate*
BARK DESCRIPTION	*Light gray and smooth when young, develops ridges and orangish-brown coloring with age*
NATIVE OR INVASIVE	*Native*

WHAT IS A MULBERRY?

The fruit of a red mulberry is highly nutritious and sweet to the taste. So, why isn't it commonly sold at the grocery store? The answer is that red mulberries are a delicate fruit with a short shelf life, making them undesirable to grow commercially.

STURDY AND SHARP

Wild honey locust trees are durable and almost completely covered in thorns! Unpleasant as that sounds, it did serve a purpose during the Civil War. Known as the "Confederate Pin Tree" to southerners, the needle-like thorns were used to pin uniforms together.

24. HONEY LOCUST

Honey locusts make their home in the central United States, where they prefer full sun and moderate irrigation. This perennial grows quickly and has an average lifespan of 100 years. Its longevity may be due to the fact that it can thrive in a variety of soil types, including alkaline soil, and grow despite the use of road salts in urban areas. While it doesn't literally produce honey, the honey locust gets its name from the sugary-tasting pulp inside its fruit. This fruit is actually an aromatic pod that is long, twisted, and brown-colored when ripe. Squirrels, raccoons, and possums are all major fans of the populus pods!

CLASSIFICATION

KINGDOM: *Plantae*

CLADE: *Tracheophytes*

CLADE: *Angiosperms*

CLADE: *Eudicots*

CLADE: *Rosids*

ORDER: *Fabales*

FAMILY: *Fabaceae*

SUBFAMILY: *Caesalpinioideae*

GENUS: *Gleditsia*

SPECIES: *G. triacanthos*

CULINARY APPLICATIONS

The fruit pods of the honey locust have numerous uses. Unripe pods are edible after being cooked, while the inner seeds taste like peas and can be cooked or eaten raw. The seeds can also be used as coffee substitutes when dried, roasted, and ground.

QUICK FACTS

TREE TYPE	*Deciduous*
LEAF ARRANGEMENT	*Alternate*
BARK DESCRIPTION	*Gray, becomes deeply furrowed with age*
NATIVE OR INVASIVE	*Native*

DOME DOMINATION

If you have visited the U.S. West Coast and enjoy entertainment, then you may be familiar with the Tacoma Dome. This unique wood-domed arena's roof was constructed using 1.6 million board feet of Douglas fir and weighs 1.444 million pounds. In addition, the wood was salvaged from a volcanic blowout of Mount St. Helens that toppled trees.

25. DOUGLAS FIR

Since the 1920s, the Douglas fir has been a popular choice for Christmas tree enthusiasts. Its soft, bluish-green needles and sweet fragrance have given it a popular following. Its native habitat covers the coastal regions of British Columbia down to central California. While the Douglas fir has historically had many uses for Native American tribes, its main application today is in construction. Of all the trees in North America, the Douglas fir yields the highest amount of timber. Hard, strong, and resilient, the wood is used for general milling and in manufacturing plywood, veneers, doors, windows, and wood flooring.

CLASSIFICATION

KINGDOM: *Plantae*

CLADE: *Tracheophytes*

CLADE: *Gymnosperms*

DIVISION: *Pinophyta*

CLASS: *Pinopsida*

ORDER: *Pinales*

FAMILY: *Pinaceae*

GENUS: *Pseudotsuga*

SPECIES: *P. menziesii*

QUICK FACTS

TREE TYPE	*Coniferous evergreen*
LEAF ARRANGEMENT	*Needles are arranged in a spiral pattern around the branchlets*
BARK DESCRIPTION	*Deeply furrowed with resin blisters*
NATIVE OR INVASIVE	*Native*

NEAT NAMESAKE

The Douglas fir was not named after a man named Douglas. His name was actually David Douglas, a famous botanist of the 19th century. His identification of the Pacific Northwest native is now cultivated worldwide.

THE GOODS AND BADS

A box elder maple has little value as a landscape tree or for lumber. Its appearance is rather plain, and its wood is both weak and brittle. While this tree lacks in some areas, it is great for pollinators since its flowers bloom early! They are also helpful near waterways, as they help prevent erosion.

26. BOX ELDER MAPLE

Box elder, or "boxelder," maple trees are very adaptable, fast-growing, medium-sized trees that can appear weedy and unkempt in the wild. While they are drought-tolerant and can thrive almost anywhere, they commonly populate floodplains, valleys, and stream banks. Also known as the "Manitoba maple," the box elder can be found from Canada in the north down to Mexico in the south. Box elders are relatively short in height and lifespan. Heights of about 50 feet are typical of the species, and they can live about 75 years. Two defining characteristics of this maple are its irregular shape and its ability to grow multiple trunks.

CLASSIFICATION

KINGDOM: *Plantae*

CLADE: *Angiosperms*

CLADE: *Eudicots*

CLADE: *Rosids*

ORDER: *Sapindales*

FAMILY: *Sapindaceae*

GENUS: *Acer*

SPECIES: *A. negundo*

QUICK FACTS

TREE TYPE	*Deciduous*
LEAF ARRANGEMENT	*Opposite*
BARK DESCRIPTION	*Light brown when young but becomes grayish-brown and grooved with age*
NATIVE OR INVASIVE	*Native*

NAME THAT TREE

It's been said that early American settlers saw the box elder maple, and its foliage reminded them of elder trees in England. In addition, the box elder wood was a whitish color, reminiscent of an evergreen shrub in the Old World called a "common box." Put "box" and "elder" together, and the box elder maple was born!

TEAMS OF TWO

Most American persimmon trees are "dioecious," meaning that there are separate male and female trees. In order to get fruit, you need to have at least one of each for fertilization. You can tell a male tree by its clusters of small flowers, while female flowers appear alone and are larger in size.

58

27. AMERICAN PERSIMMON

Most persimmons purchased at North American grocery stores are Asian persimmons. This is because they are larger and have a longer shelf life. At only 2 inches in diameter, American persimmons are delicate and difficult to transport and keep fresh. While more difficult to find, they still have many uses and are popularly eaten right off the tree. Sweeter than their Asian cousins, the American persimmon is also known as a "sugar plum" due to its candied taste and similar size to a plum. You can distinguish a ripe persimmon when it has achieved its characteristic red and golden-orange color or when it looks like it's ready to rot!

CLASSIFICATION

KINGDOM: *Plantae*

CLADE: *Angiosperms*

CLADE: *Eudicots*

CLADE: *Asterids*

ORDER: *Ericales*

FAMILY: *Ebenaceae*

GENUS: *Diospyros*

SPECIES: *D. virginiana*

QUICK FACTS

A FEW OF ITS FAVORITE THINGS

American persimmons can tolerate hot and dry conditions, but life is better for them in well-drained, moist, and sandy soils. Freezing temperatures don't bother the tree or its fruits, but they don't like to share space. They prefer ample room to grow, reaching widths of 35 feet.

TREE TYPE	*Deciduous*
LEAF ARRANGEMENT	*Alternate*
BARK DESCRIPTION	*Dark brown or gray with individual block-shaped segments*
NATIVE OR INVASIVE	*Native (originates from Kentucky)*

BERRY UNPLEASANT

Wildlife is fond of feasting on the berries of a holly tree. This, however, is not the case for humans. The berries, bark, and leaves of the holly are mildly toxic, as they contain the alkaloid "theobromine." If consumed in large quantities, it can cause vomiting and stomach issues, among other problems.

28. AMERICAN HOLLY

Sharply-tipped green leaves, a pyramidal shape, and famed red berries are the main identifiers of the American holly tree. Popular for wreath-making during the Christmas season, it is also known as "white holly" and "Christmas holly." Compared to other holly species, the American holly is the only one that can attain tree size, averaging 40 feet tall. As the tree is dioecious, male and female trees need to be in close proximity in order to produce berries. Pollinators like bees play a large role in berry production as they transfer pollen to the female trees. Unlike many tree types, the American holly bears fruit year-round.

CLASSIFICATION

KINGDOM: *Plantae*

CLADE: *Tracheophytes*

CLADE: *Angiosperms*

CLADE: *Eudicots*

CLADE: *Asterids*

ORDER: *Aquifoliales*

FAMILY: *Aquifoliaceae*

GENUS: *Ilex*

SPECIES: *I. opaca*

QUICK FACTS

TREE TYPE	*Evergreen*
LEAF ARRANGEMENT	*Alternate*
BARK DESCRIPTION	*Grayish-brown, thin, and smooth; develops a warty texture with age*
NATIVE OR INVASIVE	*Native*

DISEASE DIFFICULTY

For the most part, the gorgeous green holly tree is hardy and healthy. When sickness does come, it is usually caused by environmental factors. Too much moisture or not enough airflow are common causes of fungal disease and cankers.

EARLY DROPPERS

Don't worry if you see a California buckeye looking lackluster in the summer. Its leaf production responds to heat and water conditions. Instead of holding on until fall, leaves drop in the summer as drought conditions arise. New leaves begin to grow once the rainy season hits!

29. CALIFORNIA BUCKEYE

Compared to other North American trees, the California buckeye is on the small side. It can live up to 300 years yet only reach between 13-40 feet tall. Home to the foothill woodlands and coastal sage scrub of California, the buckeye is drought-tolerant and is the only buckeye variety in the state. Its most defining feature is the giant seed pods that hang on to their shells or drop to the ground. Smooth and chestnut-colored, the buckeyes resemble deer eyes. The downside to these giant seeds is that they, along with all parts of the tree, are toxic to both humans and animals.

CLASSIFICATION

KINGDOM: *Plantae*

CLADE: *Tracheophytes*

CLADE: *Angiosperms*

CLADE: *Eudicots*

CLADE: *Rosids*

ORDER: *Sapindales*

FAMILY: *Sapindaceae*

GENUS: *Aesculus*

SPECIES: *A. californica*

UNSUSPECTING SURPRISE

Native Californians used the roots of the California buckeye to aid in catching fish. After crushing the roots, they would throw them in slow-moving water where toxic chemicals called "saponins" would interfere with the fish's oxygen absorption. The reaction would stun the fish, making them easier to catch.

QUICK FACTS

TREE TYPE	*Deciduous*
LEAF ARRANGEMENT	*Opposite*
BARK DESCRIPTION	*Smooth and silvery gray, often coated with moss or lichen*
NATIVE OR INVASIVE	*Native*

GLOBAL SPREAD

While native to California's Central Coast, the Monterey cypress has been cultivated all over the world. One of its modern uses is for building furniture due to its durability and light weight. Being resistant to moisture damage, Monterey cypress wood has also been used to make boats, shingles, and siding.

30. MONTEREY CYPRESS

Only found in two small groves off the Pacific Ocean, the Monterey cypress is one of the rarest trees in the world. It makes its home on the Monterey Peninsula and nearby at Point Lobos. Unlike other tree species, the Monterey cypress can cope with ocean winds and salty sea spray while thriving in foggy seaside mists. Two of the defining features of the Monterey cypress are its irregular, bent shape and flat-topped canopies. Both characteristics result from the high winds that shape the tree over time. This softwood tree species can live up to 300 years and reach heights of 130 feet.

CLASSIFICATION

KINGDOM: *Plantae*

CLADE: *Tracheophytes*

CLADE: *Gymnosperms*

DIVISION: *Pinophyta*

CLASS: *Pinopsida*

ORDER: *Cupressales*

FAMILY: *Cupressaceae*

GENUS: *Hesperocyparis*

SPECIES: *H. macrocarpa*

ICONIC INTEREST

One of the most photographed trees in North America (and a Western icon) is the Lone Cypress of Pebble Beach, California. It is believed to have been born in 1750 and has weathered the elements of the Pacific Ocean atop its granite surroundings for centuries.

QUICK FACTS

TREE TYPE	*Coniferous evergreen*
LEAF ARRANGEMENT	*Opposite; shiny and flexible needle-like leaves*
BARK DESCRIPTION	*Reddish-brown, thick and fibrous*
NATIVE OR INVASIVE	*Native*

OTHER OPTIONS

Though hackberry wood does not have commercial value, this soft wood can be used as fire fuel and made into fence posts and cheap furniture. For those interested in arboriculture, the hackberry can be cultivated as a bonsai tree.

31. HACKBERRY

The hackberry is a fast-growing, medium-sized shade tree that is native to the Eastern and Midwestern United States. While it can be confused with an elm tree, the hackberry is far less susceptible to disease. A popular urban choice, hackberry trees make good street trees. They are flood- and drought-resistant while being able to tolerate air pollution and less-than-desirable soil conditions. As a result of its hardiness, it has been heralded as "one tough tree" by tree experts. Hackberry trees produce pea-sized, dark red fruit that is edible to humans but more readily consumed by birds. Thanks to the birds who help in dispersing the fruit seeds, the hackberry population is stable.

CLASSIFICATION

KINGDOM: *Plantae*

CLADE: *Tracheophytes*

CLADE: *Angiosperms*

CLADE: *Eudicots*

CLADE: *Rosids*

ORDER: *Rosales*

FAMILY: *Cannabaceae*

GENUS: *Celtis*

SPECIES: *C. occidentalis*

QUICK FACTS

TREE TYPE	*Deciduous*
LEAF ARRANGEMENT	*Alternate*
BARK DESCRIPTION	*Gray and smooth when young, develops distinctive knobby and corky bark*
NATIVE OR INVASIVE	*Native*

NUMEROUS NICKNAMES

This long-lived species has many alternate names beyond simply "hackberry." Here are a handful of other titles: "beaverwood," "nettletree," "common hackberry," "American hackberry," "northern hackberry," and "sugarberry."

67

TWO IN ONE

The American larch is a monoecious plant that grows male and female flowers. It can, therefore, self pollinate. The nickname for the pinkish female flowers is "larch roses." The wind aids in spreading the male flower pollen, which transforms the female flower into a cone.

32. AMERICAN LARCH

Also known as the "American tamarack," the American larch is a member of the pine family and the tallest of the 10 larch species around the world. While growing up to 150 feet tall, they can also live hundreds of years. One of the secrets to the tree's longevity is that it is fire-resistant in comparison to the trees it grows near. Its thick bark, up to 6 inches thick, protects its vital inner layers while the needles drop each fall. In addition, the American larch self-prunes. It drops its lower branches, which minimizes the chance of flames ascending the tree. Look for this larch in wetlands and cold climates.

CLASSIFICATION

KINGDOM: *Plantae*

CLADE: *Tracheophytes*

CLADE: *Gymnosperms*

DIVISION: *Pinophyta*

CLASS: *Pinopsida*

ORDER: *Pinales*

FAMILY: *Pinaceae*

GENUS: *Larix*

SPECIES: *L. laricina*

QUICK FACTS

AWESOME OXYMORON

Unlike most coniferous trees, the larch drops its needle-like leaves in autumn. Its needles also change color from green to yellow before they fall. A deciduous conifer sounds like an oxymoron, but it's helpful to remember that "evergreen" and "conifer" do not have the same meaning.

TREE TYPE	*Deciduous conifer*
LEAF ARRANGEMENT	*Needle-like leaves grow in clusters of 30-40 on branches*
BARK DESCRIPTION	*Reddish-brown, thick, scaly, and furrowed*
NATIVE OR INVASIVE	*Native*

PRIZED POSSESSIONS

Due to the short and contorted shape of its stumps, mountain mahogany wood is not used commercially. Instead, its wood is used to craft handmade and unique custom pieces and is prized as barbeque fuel because of its slow burn.

33. MOUNTAIN MAHOGANY

The mountain mahogany tree is a small tree or shrub that grows slowly in the foothill elevations of the Western United States. So slow is its growth that it takes about a century to reach its full height of 15-30 feet. Though not related to tropical mahogany, mountain mahogany gets its name from its dense and heavy wood that sinks in water. It is one of the longest-living known flowering trees; the oldest specimens are thought to be about 1,350 years old. Mountain mahogany trees differ from other species due to their yellow flowers that bear a small fruit with a feathery, tail-like plume.

CLASSIFICATION

KINGDOM: *Plantae*

CLADE: *Tracheophytes*

CLADE: *Angiosperms*

CLADE: *Eudicots*

CLADE: *Rosids*

ORDER: *Rosales*

FAMILY: *Rosaceae*

SUBFAMILY: *Dryadoideae*

GENUS: *Cercocarpus*

QUICK FACTS

TREE TYPE	*Deciduous to semi-evergreen*
LEAF ARRANGEMENT	*Alternate*
BARK DESCRIPTION	*Reddish-brown streaks under grayish-white grooved furrows*
NATIVE OR INVASIVE	*Native*

MINIATURE SAHARA

When you see a strand of mountain mahogany, it may remind you of a miniature African savanna. Also inhabiting dry and hot conditions, the sparsely populated mahogany has the same contorted trunk as its lookalike in Africa.

34. EASTERN COTTONWOOD

Due to their rapid growth rate, the eastern cottonwood is a popular choice for recreation sites like picnic areas and campsites. They grow tall with an extensive canopy, providing much shade. The downside to this quick expansion is that cottonwoods are more susceptible to borer pests and decay from fungal infections. Despite these deficiencies and a lack of wood durability, the eastern cottonwood has many beneficial uses. Its wood pulp is used to make high-quality paper, while the tree itself provides sturdy homes for insects, birds, and small mammals. If you seek out the cottonwood in the Eastern or Midwestern United States, you can recognize it by its deep green, triangular leaves.

CLASSIFICATION

KINGDOM: *Plantae*

CLADE: *Tracheophytes*

CLADE: *Angiosperms*

CLADE: *Eudicots*

CLADE: *Rosids*

ORDER: *Malpighiales*

FAMILY: *Salicaceae*

GENUS: *Populus*

SPECIES: *P. deltoides*

QUICK FACTS

TREE TYPE	*Deciduous*
LEAF ARRANGEMENT	*Alternate*
BARK DESCRIPTION	*Yellow-green when young, growing dark gray and furrowed with age*
NATIVE OR INVASIVE	*Native*

MESSY LEFTOVERS

Female eastern cottonwoods bear the ever-distinctive seeds with cotton-like extensions that the tree is known for. The cottony tufts or fibers are lightweight and dispersed by the wind. The end result, however, is a serious litter problem under the tree, covering large areas of ground.

73

Looking for a historic destination for your next road trip? Look no further than Fenwick, Ontario, Canada. This is the home of "The Comfort Maple," the oldest sugar maple tree, which has reached the ripe age of about 500 years. Its height is near 100 feet, with a trunk diameter of 20 feet.

35. SUGAR MAPLE

Sugar maple trees are native to the Eastern United States and Canada. Highly adaptable, it may surprise you that they can actually thrive in most of the United States, spanning sea to sea! Not only is its leaf the national emblem of Canada, but the sugar maple has commercial importance for its famous maple syrup and hardwood lumber. It is also the state tree of New York, West Virginia, Wisconsin, and Vermont. The sap of the sugar maple usually runs for 4-6 weeks in mid-February and mid-March, when daytime temperatures rise above freezing. As a heads up, it takes about 40 years for a sugar maple to grow big enough to tap for syrup!

CLASSIFICATION

KINGDOM: *Plantae*

CLADE: *Angiosperms*

CLADE: *Eudicots*

CLADE: *Rosids*

ORDER: *Sapindales*

FAMILY: *Sapindaceae*

GENUS: *Acer*

SPECIES: *A. saccharum*

QUICK FACTS

TREE TYPE	*Deciduous*
LEAF ARRANGEMENT	*Opposite*
BARK DESCRIPTION	*Smooth and gray when young, becomes scaly and irregularly furrowed with age*
NATIVE OR INVASIVE	*Native*

SAP SUPPLY

The maple syrup you buy at the store takes a lot of sap to make! Only 2-5% percent of the sap is sugar. The sap is boiled down, removing most of the water and concentrating the sweet syrup. It takes 40 gallons of sap to make 1 gallon of maple syrup. No wonder it's so expensive!

ABOUT THE
AUTHOR

Christin is the author of
several books for kids,
including many in the Little
Library of Natural History.
She lives with her family in
California, where she enjoys
rollerblading, puzzles, and a
good book.

**BUSHEL
& PECK
BOOKS**

ABOUT THE PUBLISHER

Bushel & Peck Books is a children's publishing house with a special mission. Through our Book-for-Book Promise™, we donate one book to kids in need for every book we sell. Our beautiful books are given to kids through schools, libraries, local neighborhoods, shelters, nonprofits, and also to many selfless organizations who are working hard to make a difference. So thank you for purchasing this book! Because of you, another book will find itself in the hands of a child who needs it most.

Printed in the United States
by Baker & Taylor Publisher Services